Reinhold Rost

**Trübner's Collection of Simplified Grammars**

VI. Roumanian

Reinhold Rost

**Trübner's Collection of Simplified Grammars**
*VI. Roumanian*

ISBN/EAN: 9783743394568

Manufactured in Europe, USA, Canada, Australia, Japa

Cover: Foto ©Paul-Georg Meister /pixelio.de

Manufactured and distributed by brebook publishing software (www.brebook.com)

Reinhold Rost

**Trübner's Collection of Simplified Grammars**

# TRÜBNER'S COLLECTION

OF

# SIMPLIFIED GRAMMARS

OF THE PRINCIPAL

ASIATIC AND EUROPEAN LANGUAGES.

EDITED BY

REINHOLD ROST, LL.D., Ph.D.

---

VI.

ROUMANIAN.

BY R. TORCEANU.

# CONTENTS.

|  | PAGE |
|---|---|
| ALPHABET and PRONUNCIATION | 1 |
| Phonetic Remarks | 2 |
| NOUNS: | |
| Masculine Terminations | 7 |
| The Plural of Masculine Nouns | 7 |
| Feminine Terminations | 8 |
| The Plural of Feminine Nouns | 9 |
| Neuter Nouns | 10 |
| The Accent, or Intonation | 10 |
| THE ARTICLE | 11 |
| The Masculine Article | 12 |
| The Feminine Article | 13 |
| Cases of Nouns | 14 |
| ADJECTIVES: | |
| Formation of the Feminine from the Masculine | 16 |
| Relation of Substantive and Adjective | 17 |
| Comparison | 18 |
| Numerals | 18 |
| Ordinal Numbers | 20 |
| Proportional Numbers | 21 |

## CONTENTS.

PRONOUNS :                                                                PAGE
   Personal Pronouns . . . . . . . 21
      Singular . . . . . . . . 21
      Plural . . . . . . . . 22
   The Abbreviated Forms of the Genitive and Dative . 22
      Singular . . . . . . . . 22
      Plural . . . . . . . . 23
   The Reflexive Pronouns . . . . . . 23
      Masculine . . . . . . . . 23
      Feminine . . . . . . . 24
   Possessive Pronouns . . . . . . 24
   Demonstrative Pronouns . . . . . . 25
   Interrogative and Relative Pronouns . . . . 25
   Indeterminate Pronouns . . . . . . 26

VERBS :
   Auxiliary Verbs . . . . . . . 26
   Terminations of Verbs . . . . . . 33
   The Accent of Verbs . . . . . . 49
   The Passive Voice . . . . . . . 50
      The Reflexive Forms . . . . . . 51
   Irregular Verbs . . . . . . . 54
   Impersonal Verbs . . . . . . 57

ADVERBS . . . . . . . . 57
PREPOSITIONS . . . . . . . . 59
CONJUNCTIONS and INTERJECTIONS . . . . 60

SYNTAX . . . . . . . . . 61

# PREFACE.

THERE is hardly a language, or even a dialect, to be found unworthy of the philologist's attention. The Roumanian tongue can claim that attention on more grounds than one. It is the language of an European country as independent as England itself, and is spoken by a population numbering eight millions of souls, extending beyond the bounds of Roumania itself into Bulgaria, Servia, Transylvania, Hungary, the Austrian province of the Bukovina, and the Russian province of Bessarabia. These are the people who speak the Roumanian proper, the language whose Grammar is treated of in the following pages, called also, for the sake of distinction, the Northern or Daco-Rouman. A closely allied dialect known as the Southern or Macedo-Rouman is spoken by a scattered population of about half a million, in Macedonia, Thessaly, and the adjoining highlands of Albania. The popular element it contains is rightly considered a rich treasure by philologists and students of folk-lore. The Roumanian Language owes its origin and distinctive character to the influx of heterogeneous words and expressions into "the rustic Latin" spoken by the Roman provincials between Pontus and Adria. These provincials became barbarized in consequence of the protracted miseries induced by the repeated invasions of the northern barbarians. The western portion of the Roman Empire was conquered once for all by the Teutonic invaders. The lands north and south of the eastern course of the Danube were repeatedly laid waste for many centuries by successive waves of barbarians—Goths and Huns, Slavs and Bulgars. This unsettled state of things, though disastrous for the political and social development of the Roumanian people, rendered possible the growth of an original language differing in a marked manner from the other Romance languages of the West.

I have endeavoured in this short Grammar to give the student a clear notion of the framework of the Roumanian Language, and to help him in becoming acquainted with it without unnecessary consumption of his time. Any elucidatory details which may be considered not absolutely indispensable in a strictly philological handbook will nevertheless, it is hoped, prove useful to those who learn the language for some practical purpose.

R. TORCEANU.

London,
*September*, 1883.

# ROUMANIAN GRAMMAR.

## Alphabet and Pronunciation.

The Roumanian Alphabet consists of the following letters:—

A, a, as *a* in *father*.
B, b, as in English.
C, c, before *e* and *i* as *ch* in *cheese*, softer than in English: otherwise as *k*.
D, d, as in English.
D̦, d̦, like *z*.
E, e, as *é* in French, sometimes as *ye* in *yet*.
F, f, as in English.
G, g, hard, as in *gum*, but before *e* and *i* like *j* in *joke*.
H, h, guttural, as *ch* in *loch*.
I, i, as in *police*.
J, j, as in French *jour*.
K, k, as in English.
L, l, „ „
M, m, „ „
N, n, „ „
O, o, „ „
P, p, „ „
R, r, a rolling *r*.
S, s, as in English.
Ș, ș, as *sh* in *ship*.
T, t, softer than in English.
Ț, ț, as *ts*, or like the German *z* in *zeit*.
U, u, as *oo* in *tool*.
V, v, as *v* in English.
X, x, as *x* „ „
Y, y, as *i* in the English word *king*.
Z, z, as in English.

B

ŭ, ĕ and ŏ are pronounced like the Russian ы, or nearly like the English *u* in *murder*. The vowels in this case make no difference in the pronunciation, but represent only the derivation of the word. Thus, in *bländ*, which is from the Latin *blandus*, *a* is used in preference to any of the other vowels. Similar reasons govern the orthography of words from Slavonic and other sources.

ŭ, when it occurs at the end of a word, is pronounced like a silent *u*, which is called ŭ short.

ó and é are pronounced as if followed by *a*: *mórte*, pronounced *moarte*; *pétră*, pronounced *peatră*. But at the end of words these diphthongs are to be written *ea*, *oa*.

ĭ, at the end of a word, is pronounced generally as a silent *i*, which is called ĭ short.

î: this is generally confounded in writing with ĭ, but has a very different sound, approaching the French nasal vowel *un*.

*e* is pronounced like the French *é* in *fermé*; but at the beginning of words, except in the case of neologisms, and occasionally in the middle, *e* is pronounced like *ye* in *yet*— e.g., *el era*, 'he was.' This peculiarity is of Slavonic origin.

*s*. When *s* occurs between two vowels it is pronounced as in English *z*. Sometimes it retains its original sound, as in *casa*, but some modern writers spell such words with a double *s*.

## Phonetic Remarks.

One of the greatest difficulties which the Roumanian language presents to foreigners is the difficulty of learning and remembering the nice modifications of sound to which certain letters (both vowels and consonants) are subject. It

## PHONETIC REMARKS.

is impossible, however, in the present space to specify all such modifications, and we must content ourselves with the following hints, which will be of service to the student.

**a.)**

1. *a*, in an accented syllable, becomes *ă*, so soon as that syllable becomes through inflection unaccented:

eŭ *tac*, 'I am silent;'   eŭ *tăcuĭ*, 'I was silent.'
*el tace*, 'He is silent;'   *tăcere*, 'silence' (*noun*).
*barbă*, 'beard;'   *bărbat*, 'man.'
etc.

2. *a* becomes *ă* in the plural of many words, even though the accentuation is unchanged:

*carte*, 'book;'   *cărțĭ*, 'books.'
*parte*, 'part;'   *părțĭ*,
*ogradă*, 'yard;'   *ogrădĭ*,
*sabie*, 'sword;'   *săbiĭ*,
etc.

**e.**

*e* is often modified into *ĕ* in the singular of nouns and in the conjugation of verbs:

*pĕr*,   'hair;'   *perĭ*.
*rĕŭ*,   'bad;'   *reĭ*.
*mĕr*,   'apple;'   *mere*.
*a vede*,   'to see;'   eŭ *vĕd*, 'I see.'
eŭ *vĕduĭ*, 'I saw;'   *vĕdĕnd*, 'seeing.'
etc.

*Note.*—There is one case in which *e* changes into *i*, viz. in the verb *a veni*, 'to come,' where *e* becomes *i* whenever the accent is upon it :

 eŭ *vin*, 'I come;' *el vine*, 'he comes;' *vină*, 'come.'

### i.

*i* becomes *î* long in the singulars of some nouns, and in the root syllable of certain persons of the verbs :

| | | | |
|---|---|---|---|
| *mormînt*, | 'grave;' | *morminte*, | 'graves.' |
| *sfînt*, | 'saint;' | *sfinți*, | 'saints.' |
| *cuvînt*, | 'word;' | *cuvinte*, | 'words.' |
| *tînĕr*, | 'youth;' | *tineri*, | 'youths.' |
| eŭ *vînd*, | 'I sell;' | *tu vindi, el vinde*, etc. |

### o.

Sometimes *o* is changed into *u* when the syllable in which it stands becomes unaccented :

| | | | |
|---|---|---|---|
| *joc*, | 'play;' | *jucărie*, | 'toy.' |
| eŭ *port*, | 'I wear;' | eŭ *purtam*, | 'I wore.' |
| eŭ *rog*, | 'I pray;' | eŭ *rugam*, | 'I prayed.' |
| | *rugăciune*, | 'prayer.' |
| eŭ *sbor*, | 'I fly.' | eŭ *sburam*, | 'I flew.' |

       etc.

More important than any of the foregoing modifications of sounds are those of *e* and *o* into the diphthongs *é* (ea), *ó* (oa), in which the stress falls on the *a*.

### e.

*e* changes into *é* (ea) generally when it is accented in a word, and when an affix containing the vowel *a* or *ă* has to be added :

  *acest,* 'this;'   *acéstă* (fem.), *acésta.*
  *drept,* 'upright;' *dréptă*   ,,   *drépta,* etc.

With some of the words which have had the *e* modified into *é* the sound of *e* has subsequently disappeared; thus—

 *fétă,* plur. *fete* (girls), is pronounced and written *fată.*
 *méssă,*  ,,   *messe* (tables),  ,,  ,,   *massă.*
 *vétră,*  ,,   *vetre* (hearths),  ,,  ,,   *vatră.*
 *véră,*  ,,   *vere* (cousins),  ,,  ,,   *vară.*
       etc.

It is only by the plural that we discover that the *a* of the singular is a modification of *e*.

## O.

*o* changes into *ó* (*oa*) when we affix to the word in which it occurs accented, a syllable containing one of the vowels *a*, *ă* or *e* :

  *eŭ port,*  'I wear;'   *el pórtŭ,* 'he wears.'
  *pórte (el),* 'let him wear' (*imperat*).
  *frumos,*  'handsome,'   *frumóssă, frumóssa.*
      etc.

*Note.*—This modification is not made in imported words, or in neologisms :

  *onest,* 'honest;'   *onestă.*
  *chines,*     *chinesă.*
  *engles,*     *englesă.*
  *eŭ onor,* 'I honour;' *el onoră,* 'he honours.'

It is impossible, however, to attempt to alter those cases in which the passage from *e* to *é* and from *o* to *ó* are time honoured.

### d, t, s.

*D*, *s*, and *t*, at the end of words to which an *ĭ* has been affixed, change respectively into *ḍ*, *ṣ*, *ṭ* :

  *eŭ cred*,   'I believe ;'   *tu creḍĭ*.
  *brad*,    'fir-tree ;'    *braḍĭ*.
  *eŭ cos*,    'I sew ;'    *tu coṣĭ*
  *eŭ socot*,   'I think ;'    *tu socoṭĭ*, etc.

If the word ends in *st*, the *s* alone undergoes modification :

  *acest*, 'this ;'   *aceṣtĭ*, 'these.'
  *onest*, 'honest ;' *oneṣtĭ* (*plural*).

With verbs this change occurs sometimes before *u*, *ĕ*, *i* :

  *eŭ vĕd*, 'I see ;' *eŭ vĕḍuĭ*, 'I saw.'
  *vĕḍĕnd*, 'seeing ;' etc.

Euphony occasionally requires that certain letters should be (1) omitted from, (2) interpolated in, or (3) affixed to a word :

  (1) *cale*,   'road ;'   *căĭ* (*plural* for *călĭ*).
     *viṭel*,   'calf ;'   *viṭeĭ* (*plur. f. viṭelĭ*).
 *eŭ vin*, 'I come ;' *tu viĭ*, 'thou comest ;' for *tu vinĭ*.
*tu saĭ*, 'thou leapest ;' for *tu sarĭ*, etc.

  (2) *om-u-luĭ*, 'to the man ;' for *omluĭ*.
     *veni-u-ar*, 'should he come ;' for *veni-ar*.
       etc.

  (3) *îmĭ vine reŭ*, 'I feel ill ;' for *mi vine reŭ*.

# Nouns (Nume).

## MASCULINE TERMINATIONS.

The determination of the gender of the noun is one of the difficulties of the Roumanian language. The student, however, must first observe that masculine nouns generally end in a consonant:

| | |
|---|---|
| *Român,* | 'Roumanian.' |
| *Engles,* | 'Englishman.' |
| *Grec,* | 'Greek.' |
| *nepot,* | 'nephew.' |
| *professor,* | 'teacher.' |
| *împărat,* | 'emperor.' |
| *tun,* | 'cannon.' |

There are, however, a few masculine nouns which end with a vowel, and here the real difficulty begins. They will generally be found to end in—

e short: *rege,* 'king;' *pește,* 'fish;' *frate,* 'brother.'
u or ŭ: *socru,* 'father-in-law;' *Dumnezeŭ,* 'God.'
ĭ short: *usturoĭ,* 'onion;' *ciocoĭ,* 'parvenu.'
ă short: *tată,* 'father;' *popă,* 'priest.'

## *The Plural of Masculine Nouns.*

The plurals of all masculine nouns without exception end in ĭ short. This ĭ is added to the singular when the singular ends in a consonant. When it ends in a vowel, that vowel is changed into ĭ. When the singular ends in ĭ, no change is made:

| | | | |
|---|---|---|---|
| pom, | 'fruit tree;' | pomĭ, | 'fruit trees.' |
| tălhar, | 'thief;' | tălharĭ, | 'thieves.' |
| impărat, | 'emperor;' | impăraţĭ, | 'emperors.' |
| rege, | 'king;' | regĭ, | 'kings.' |
| peste, | 'fish;' | peştĭ, | 'fishes.' |
| frate, | 'brother;' | fraţĭ, | 'brothers.' |
| socru, | 'father-in-law;' | socrĭ, | 'fathers-in-law.' |
| Dumnezeŭ, | 'God;' | Dumnezeĭ, | 'Gods.' |
| tată, | 'father:' | taţĭ, | 'fathers.' |
| popă, | 'priest;' | popĭ, | 'priests.' |
| ciocoĭ, | 'parvenu;' | ciocoĭ, | 'parvenus.' |

*Note* I.—If *cal*, 'horse,' has for plural *caĭ*, this is done for the sake of euphony.

*Note* II.—*Om*, 'man,' has its plural *ómenĭ* (homines); *nume*, 'noun,' *numenĭ*; but *nume* also is more generally used for the plural.

## Feminine Terminations.

As masculine nouns generally end with a consonant, so feminine nouns generally end with the vowel ă:

| | |
|---|---|
| Romănă, | 'Roumanian' (*f.*) |
| Englesă, | 'Englishwoman.' |
| Grécă, | 'Greek woman.' |
| nepótă, | 'niece.' |
| professóră, | 'teacher' (*f.*). |
| împărătéssă, | 'empress.' |
| cassă, | 'house.' |
| miréssă, | 'bride.' |

## FEMININE TERMINATIONS.

There are feminine nouns also which end with the vowels:

*e* short: *ca*r*te*, 'book;' *pă*n*e*, 'bread;' *cu*r*te*, 'court.'
*a* long: *ba*s*ma*, 'handkerchief;' *pa*ra 'farthing.'
*e* long: *ste*, 'star;' *bele*, 'grievance.'

### The Plural of Feminine Nouns.

There are several ways in which the feminine plural is formed.
Nouns ending in *ă* make their plural by changing *ă* into *e*:

| | | | |
|---|---|---|---|
| *ma*m*ă*, | 'mother;' | *ma*m*e*, | 'mothers.' |
| *d*ó*mnă*, | 'lady;' | *d*ó*mne*, | 'ladies.' |
| *co*p*ilă*, | 'girl;' | *co*p*ile*, | 'girls.' |
| *re*g*ină*, | 'queen;' | *re*g*ine*, | 'queens.' |

Those ending in *e* short, take *ĭ* in the plnral:

| | | | |
|---|---|---|---|
| *ca*r*te*, | 'book;' | *că*r*țĭ*, | 'books.' |
| *pă*n*e*, | 'bread;' | *pă*n*ĭ*, | 'breads.' |
| *cu*r*te*, | 'court;' | *cu*r*țĭ*, | 'courts.' |

Those ending in *a* long, add the particle *le* to the singular:

| | | | |
|---|---|---|---|
| *ba*s*ma*, | 'handkerchief;' | *ba*s*male*, | 'handkerchiefs.' |
| *pa*ra, | 'farthing;' | *pa*ra*le*, | 'money or farthings.' |

Those ending in *e* long (pronounced *ea*, *é* in the singular), and *zi* (the only word ending in *i* long), add also *le* for the plural:

| | | | |
|---|---|---|---|
| *ste*, | 'star;' | *stele*, | 'stars.' |
| *că*ț*e*, | 'bitch;' | *că*ț*ele*, | 'bitches.' |
| *nu*e, | 'rod;' | *nu*e*le*, | 'rods.' |
| *z*i, | 'day;' | *z*i*le*, | 'days.' |

*Note.*—If *va*c*ă*, 'cow,' has for plural *va*c*ĭ*; *so*r*ă*, 'sister,' *so*r*ĭ*; *ca*l*e*, 'way,' *că*ĭ, this is done for the sake of euphony.

## Neuter Nouns.

But there are greater difficulties than these with which we have to deal. There are in the Roumanian language nouns which though masculine in the singular become feminine in the plural. This plural ends in *e* or *urĭ*:

| | | | |
|---|---|---|---|
| *pal*at, | 'palace;' | *pal*ate, | 'palaces.' |
| *pod*, | 'bridge;' | *pod*urĭ, | 'bridges.' |
| *fol*os, | 'advantage;' | *fol*ósse, | 'advantages.' |

Many nouns belong to this class, and they can be learnt only by long practice.

---

To sum up what has already been said :—Masculine nouns generally end with a consonant; there are a few exceptions which end in *e, ŭ, ĭ*, and *ă*. All masculine nouns end in *ĭ* in the plural.

Feminine nouns end for the most part in *ă*, which in the plural is changed to *e*. A few end in *e* short, which in the plural becomes *ĭ*. Those nouns which end in *a* long, *e* long, and *i* long, form their plural by the addition of *le* to the final letter.

There are also nouns masculine in the singular, and feminine in the plural, this plural ending in *e* or *urĭ*.

## *The Accent or Intonation.*

Having treated of the terminations of masculine and feminine nouns, we come next to speak of the different particles affixed to nouns, which vary according to the gender and the ending of the nouns.

But before showing systematically these variations of the particles, we must apprise the student that for the sake of euphony a vowel will sometimes be placed between the noun and the particle, so that the noun will receive the addition of one or more syllables. The foreigner will often be surprised to find a noun thus changed from a monosyllable to a word of three, four, or five syllables, and will find it difficult to discover the accented syllable of such a word.

To make his task easier, let him remember that the *intonation* of the word remains *unchanged*, that the accented syllable of the word keeps its accent by whatever number of syllables the word has been lengthened.

*Note.*—The only exception is when we affix diminutives or augmentatives to the nouns, in which case the accent falls upon those particles :

| | |
|---|---|
| Román, | 'Roumanian.' |
| Romănuluĭ, | 'to the Roumanian.' |
| Romănilor, | 'to the Roumanians.' |
| raționament, | 'reasoning.' |
| raționamentelor, | 'of the reasonings.' |
| capăt, | 'extremity.' |
| capetelor, | 'of the extremity.' |
| capătuluĭ, | 'to the extremities.' |

## The Article.

The word answering to the English article 'the' varies according as it is used for the singular or the plural, for masculine or feminine nouns, and even for masculine nouns of different terminations; one form being used for a noun ending with a consonant, another for that whose final letter is a vowel, the differences between vowel and vowel even necessitating a different form of the article.

## The Masculine Article.

The masculine nouns ending with a consonant take the article *l* preceded by *u*; thus:

| | | | |
|---|---|---|---|
| o*m*, | 'man;' | o*m-u-l*, | 'the man.' |
| ca*l*, | 'horse;' | ca*l-u-l*, | 'the horse.' |
| *tun*, | 'cannon;' | *tun-u-l*, | 'the cannon.' |
| tă*lh*ar, | 'thief;' | tă*lh*ar-*u-l*, | 'the thief.' |
| *pĕr*, | 'hair;' | *pĕr-u-l*, | 'the hair.' |

It is easy to see that in these words the vowel *u* is interpolated for the sake of euphony; for it is disagreeable to the ear of a Roumanian to pronounce o*ml*, *tunl*, *focl*, *pĕrl*, *tălharl*, as in the English words 'people,' 'little,' 'nimble.'

When a masculine noun ends with *u* there is no occasion to insert another *u*, and so the definite noun will be—

| | | | |
|---|---|---|---|
| *socru*, | 'father-in-law;' | *socru-l*, | 'the father-in-law.' |
| *leŭ*, | 'lion;' | *leu-l*, | 'the lion.' |

The masculine nouns ending with *e* take the article *le*:

| | | | |
|---|---|---|---|
| *rege*, | 'king;' | *rege-le*, | 'the king.' |
| *frate*, | 'brother;' | *frate-le*, | 'the brother.' |
| *munte*, | 'mountain;' | *munte-le*, | 'the mountain.' |

Those ending in *ĭ* follow the rule of those ending with a consonant:

| | | | |
|---|---|---|---|
| *ustu*roĭ, | 'onion;' | *usturoi-u-l*, | 'the onion.' |
| *cioc*oĭ, | 'parvenu;' | *ciocoi-u-l*, | 'the parvenu.' |

Those ending in *ă* change the *ă* in *a*, following the analogy of feminine nouns:

| | | | |
|---|---|---|---|
| *ta*tă, | 'father;' | *ta*ta, | 'the father.' |
| *po*pă, | 'priest;' | *po*pa, | 'the priest.' |

We have seen that in the plural all masculine nouns end in ĭ. The plural bearing the article will be shown by adding a second ĭ, whereby the former ĭ becomes long *i*:

| | | | |
|---|---|---|---|
| *Români*, | 'Roumanians;' | *Românii*, | 'the Roumanians.' |
| *pomĭ*, | 'fruit-trees;' | *pomiĭ*, | 'the fruit trees.' |
| *regĭ*, | 'kings;' | *regiĭ*, | 'the kings.' |
| *socrĭ*, | 'father-in-law;' | *socriĭ*, | 'fathers-in-law.' |
| *dumnezeĭ*, | 'gods;' | *dumnezeiĭ*, | 'the gods.' |
| *popĭ*, | 'priests;' | *popiĭ*, | 'the priests.' |
| *ciocoĭ*, | 'parvenus;' | *ciocoiĭ*, | 'the parvenus.' |
| *caĭ*, | 'horses;' | *caiĭ*, | 'the horses.' |

*Note.*—*Copĭl*, 'boy,' has the plural *copiĭ*, by the omission of *l*; the articled noun will be of course *copiiĭ*; thus, *fiŭ*, 'son,' *fiĭ*, 'sons,' *fiiĭ*, 'the sons.'

## The Feminine Article.

The article is expressed in the feminine by an affixed *a*, but how this is done depends upon the final letter of the noun itself.

A noun ending in ă will change ă into *a*:

| | | | |
|---|---|---|---|
| *Românӑ*, | 'Roumanian;' | *Românа*, | 'the Rouman.' |
| *nepótӑ*, | 'niece;' | *nepóta*, | 'the niece.' |
| *professórӑ*, | 'teacher;' | *professóra*, | 'the teacher.' |
| *cassӑ*, | 'house;' | *cassa*, | 'the house.' |
| *miréssӑ*, | 'bride;' | *miréssa*, | 'the bride.' |

Those ending in *e* do not change this *e*, but add the letter *a* to it; thus—

| | | | |
|---|---|---|---|
| *carte*, | 'book;' | *cartea*, | 'the book.' |
| *păne*, | 'bread;' | *pănea*, | 'the bread.' |
| *curte*, | 'court;' | *curtea*, | 'the court.' |

Those which end with *a, e* or *i* long, add the particle *a* to the final vowel, inserting *u* for the sake of euphony:

  basma, 'handkerchief;' basma-u-a, 'the handkerchief.'
  sté, 'star;'   stéua, 'the star.'
  belé, 'grievance;' beléua, 'the grievance.'
  zi, 'day;'   ziua, 'the day.'

Feminine nouns, as we have seen, form their plurals in several ways—nouns which end in *ă* changing the *ă* into *e* in the plural, those ending in *e* changing the *e* into *ĭ*, those ending with *a, e* and *i* long all adding the particle *le* in the plural. In all cases the plural definite article is formed by the addition of *le*:

  casse, 'houses;'  cassele, 'the houses.'
  cărţĭ, 'books;'  cărţile, 'the books.'
  basmale, 'handkerchiefs;' basmalele, 'the handkerchiefs.'
  stele, 'stars;'  stelele, 'the stars.'

### Cases of Nouns.

Roumanian grammarians usually arrange the cases as follows:

| Nominative. | Dative. |
| Vocative. | Accusative. |
| Genitive. | Ablative. |

We have already seen the nominative case, this being the noun with or without the article.

The vocative case for the masculine ends in *e* for the singular, and *lor* for the plural; to the feminine *o* for the singular, and *lor* for the plural:

  om, 'man;' omule, ómenilor.
  copilă, 'girl;' copilo, copilelor.

## CASES OF NOUNS.

The genitives of masculine nouns are formed by the addition of the particle *luĭ* in the singular and *lor* in the plural, placing *a* before the nouns :—

    *a omuluĭ*, 'of the man ;'   *a ómenilor*, 'of the men.'
    *a leuluĭ*, 'of the lion ;'    *a leilor*,    'of the lions.'

For feminine nouns we change the final vowel into *eĭ* in the singular, and add *lor* to the plural:

    *a copileĭ*, 'of the girl ;'   *a copilelor*, 'of the girls.'
    *a Regineĭ*, 'of the Queen ;'  *a Reginelor*, 'of the Queens.'

The dative, singular and plural, are formed in the same way, but without the addition of *a*:

    *omuluĭ*,  'to the man ;'   *ómenilor*,  'to the men.'
    *leuluĭ*,   'to the lion ;'    *leilor*,     'to the lions.'
    *copileĭ*,  'to the girl ;'    *copilelor*,  'to the girls.'
    *Regineĭ*,  'to the Queen ;'  *Reginelor*,  'to the Queens.'

The accusative is like the nominative, but with the addition of the preposition *pe* placed before the noun in the case of animate beings :

    *pe om* or *pe omul*, *pe ómenĭ* or *pe ómeniĭ*.
    *pe regină* or *pe regina*, *pe regine* or *pe reginele*.

The ablative is expressed by the nominative, preceded by one of the following prepositions : *în, la, din, de la,* etc.

*Note.*—The masculine nouns ending with *ă* in their cases follow the analogy of feminine nouns.

Masculine proper nouns do not take generally the definite article, and the particles marking the genitive and dative are placed before them :

    *Gheorghe*,         'George.'
    *a luĭ Gheorghe*,   'of George.'
    *luĭ Gheorghe*,     'to George.'

Feminine proper nouns follow the same rule as feminine common nouns.

## Adjectives (Agective).

After what has been previously said concerning the nouns, it will be found easy to understand the declination of adjectives, whose modifications of gender, number and case are regulated by the same rules as apply to nouns.

*Formation of the Feminine from the Masculine.*

Before proceeding to explain the use of adjectives in relation to nouns substantive, a few words must be said concerning the derivation of the feminine gender from the masculine.

The masculine gender, when it ends with a consonant, turned into the feminine by the addition of ă; as—

   bu*n*,  'good;'  bună.
   na*l*t,  'high;'  naltă.
   fru*m*os, 'beautiful;' frumóssă.
        etc.

Those ending with u or ŭ change that vowel into ă:

   ne*g*ru, 'black;' négră.
   a*s*pru, 'rough;' aspră.
   noŭ,  'new;'  noă.
   ebreŭ, 'Hebrew;' ebreă.

A few of those ending in ŭ preceded by e, change that ŭ into a long in the feminine:

   greŭ, 'heavy;' grea.
   rĕŭ,  'bad;'  rea.

# ADJECTIVES.

Those ending with *ŭ* preceded by *i* change that *ŭ* into *e*:

  *viŭ,*  'living;'  *vie.*
  *vișiniŭ,* 'cherry-coloured;' *vișinie,* etc.

Those ending in *e* remain unchanged in the feminine.

### Relation of Substantive and Adjective.

In general use the adjectives follow the nouns:

  *ziua bună,* '(the) good day.'
  *séra bună,* '(the) good evening.'
  *nópte bună,* 'good night.'

In this case the substantive alone is declined, while the adjective takes no modification except the mark of number:

| | | | |
|---|---|---|---|
| *om bun,* | 'good man;' | *ómeni buni,* | 'good men.' |
| *a omuluĭ bun,* | 'of the good man;' | *a ómenilor buni,* | 'of the good men.' |
| *omuluĭ bun,* | 'to the good man.' | *ómenilor buni,* | 'to the good men.' |

      etc.

The only exception is in the case of feminine adjectives, whose form in the genitive and dative singular depart a little from that of the nominative:

  *cassă bună,* 'good house;' *casse bune.*
  *a casseĭ bune,*    *a casselor bune.*
  *casseĭ bune,*     *casselor bune.*

When the noun takes the article, the adjective can be preceded by the demonstrative *cel* (feminine *cea*), 'this,' 'that.' This takes all the modifications of gender, number and case, but should be omitted in translation into English:

  *omul cel bun,*  *cassa cea bună.*
  *a omuluĭ celuĭ bun,* *a casseĭ celeĭ bune,* etc.

But the adjective may stand also before the noun. When it does so the rules are inverted; it is then the adjective that takes all the modifications, whereas the noun remains unchanged, save in the feminine genitive and dative singular, and in the plural:

| | |
|---|---|
| bunul om, | buniĭ ómenĭ. |
| a bunuluĭ om, | a bunilor ómenĭ. |
| bunuluĭ om, | bunilor ómenĭ. |
| etc. | |
| buna cassă, | bunele casse. |
| a buneĭ casse, | a bunelor casse. |
| buneĭ casse, | bunelor casse. |
| etc. | |

*Note.*—The use of the determinative *cel* and *cea* when the adjective precedes the substantive is more common in verse than prose.

## Comparison.

The comparison is formed by placing before the adjective the particle *maĭ* (*magis*) for the comparative, and *cel maĭ* for the superlative:

omul bun,    maĭ bun,    cel maĭ bun.

## Numerals.

The following is a list of the names of numerals:—

1. *un* (masc.), u*na* or *o* (fem.)
2. *doĭ*   ,,   *doă* (fem.)
3. *treĭ*.
4. *patru*.
5. *cincĭ*.
6. *şesse*.
7. *şepte*.
8. *opt*.

## NUMERALS.

9. nouă.
10. zece.
11. un-spre-zecé (one after ten).
12. doĭ-spre-zece.
13. treĭ „ „
14. patru „ „
15. cincĭ „ „
16. șesse „ „
17. șepte „ „
18. opt „ „
19. nouă „ „
20. doă zecĭ.
21. doă zecĭ și un (twenty and one).
22. doă zecĭ și doĭ.
23. „ „ treĭ.
24. „ „ patru.
25. „ „ cincĭ.
26. „ „ șesse.
27. „ „ șepte.
28. „ „ opt.
29. „ „ nouă.
30. treĭ zecĭ.
31. treĭ zecĭ și un.
32. „ „ doĭ.
33. „ „ treĭ.
34. „ „ patru.
35. „ „ cincĭ.
36. „ „ șesse.

37. treĭ zecĭ și șepte.
38. „ „ opt.
39. „ „ nouă.
40. patru zecĭ.
50. cincĭ „
60. șesse „
70. șepte „
80. opt „
90. nouă „
100. o sută (sometimes una sută).
101. o sută un.
102. „ doĭ.
103. „ treĭ.
104. „ patru.
105. „ cincĭ.
110. „ zece.
115. „ cincĭ-spre-zece.
200. doă sute.
300. treĭ „
400. patru „
500. cincĭ „
600. șesse „
700. șepte „
800. opt „
900. nouă „
1000. o mie (sometimes una mie).
2000. doă miĭ.
1,000,000. un milion, etc.

(1.) The numerals 1 and 2 have the masculine and

the feminine form; so also has 3 (*treĭ*), but rarely *trele*.
U*n*, u*na*, is declinable, and serves as the indefinite article:

 *Te-a̯ căutat un domn*,  'A gentleman called on you.'
 U*nĭĭ ómenĭ*,     'Some people (men).'

(2.) The following numerals have a second, abbreviated, form.

| | | | | |
|---|---|---|---|---|
| 11 | u*nsprece.* | | 17 | *septsprece.* |
| 12 | *doĭsprece.* | | 18 | *optsprece.* |
| 13 | *treĭsprece.* | | 19 | *nouăsprece.* |
| 14 | *paĭsprece.* | | 50 | *cinzecĭ.* |
| 15 | *cinsprece.* | | 60 | *seĭzecĭ.* |
| 16 | *şeĭsprece.* | | | |

(3.) Fractions are expressed by the affix *ime*:

 *treime*, 'third;'  *pătrime*, 'quarter;' etc.

*Ordinal Numbers.*

The Ordinal Number for u*n* is *întăĭ*. The other Ordina Numbers are formed by affixing the particle *le* in masculine and *a* in feminine, and placing before the numbers the particle *al* in the first, and *a* in the second case:

| | | |
|---|---|---|
| 1 | *întăĭ* or *al* u*nule,* | *a* u*na.* |
| 2 | *al doile,* | *a doa.* |
| 3 | *al treile,* | *a treia.* |
| 4 | *al patrule,* | *a patra.* |
| 5 | *al cincile,* | *a cincea.* |
| 12 | *al doĭsprezecile,* | *a doăsprezecea.* |
| 20 | *al doăzecile,* | *a doăzecea.* |
| 21 | *al doăzecĭ şi* u*nule,* | *a doăzecĭ si una.* |

      etc.

*Proportional Numbers.*

For these numbers two forms are used, one of Latin origin:

1. *simplu,* 2. *duplu,* 3. *triplu,* etc.

The other is formed by affixing *it* to the cardinal number and prefixing to it the particle *in:*

1 *simplu,*
2 *îndoit, îndoită.*
3 *întreit, întreită.*

4 *împătrit, împătrită.*
100 *însutit, însutită.*
1000 *înmiit, înmiită.*

etc.

## Pronouns (Pronume).

### Personal Pronouns.

The personal pronouns are:

Eŭ, 'I;' *tu,* 'thou;' *el* (masc.), *ea* (fem.), 'he,' 'she.'

*Note.*—Eŭ, *el, ea,* are pronounced as if written *yeŭ, yel, yea*

They are declined as follows:—

*Singular.*

Nom. Eŭ, 'I;' *tu,* 'thou;' *el, ea,* 'he,' 'she.'

Dat. *mie,* 'to me;' *ţie,* 'to thee;' *luĭ, eĭ,* 'to him,' 'to her.'

Acc. *pe mine,* 'me;' *pe tine,* 'thee;' *pe el, pe ea,* 'him,' 'her.'

*Plural.*

Nom. *Noĭ*, 'we;'    *voĭ*, 'you;'    *eĭ, ele*, 'they.'
Dat. *nouă*, 'to us;'    *vouă*, 'to you;'    *lor*, 'them.'
Acc. *pe noĭ*,    *pe voĭ*,    *pe eĭ, pe ele.*

The genitive is replaced by the possessive pronouns.

For the Vocative and Ablative cases we use different interjections or prepositions, followed by the Dative or Accusative. (See Syntax.)

For the third person, instead of e*l*, *ea*, the pronouns, *dînsul, dînsa*, are often used.

*The Abbreviated Forms of the Genitive and Dative.*

We have an abbreviated form of the personal pronouns the right use of which is very difficult for foreigners to acquire.

*Singular.*

DATIVE.

Instead of *mie* :    instead of *ţie* :    instead of *luĭ* or *eĭ* :
   *mi*,    *ţi*,    *i*,
   -*mĭ*,    -*ţĭ*,    -*ĭ*,
   *mĭ*-,    *ţĭ*-,    *ĭ*-,
   îm*ĭ*.    îţĭ.    îĭ.

ACCUSATIVE.

Instead of *mine* :    instead of *tine* :    instead of *el, ea* :
   *mĕ*.    *te*.    -*l, o*,
                                  *l', o*,
                                    *il, o.*

## REFLEXIVE PRONOUNS.

*Plural.*

### DATIVE.

Instead of *nouĕ* :  instead of *vouĕ* :  instead of *lor* :
ne or *ni*.   *vĕ* or *vi*.   *le* or *li*.

### ACCUSATIVE.

Instead of *pe noĭ* :  instead of *pe voĭ* :  instead of *pe eĭ* or *ele* :
ne.   *vĕ*.   -*ĭ*,
    *ĭ*-, or *le*,
    *iĭ*.

Both forms of the personal pronouns are often used in one and the same sentence :

| | |
|---|---|
| I*mĭ* trebue mie, | 'I want.' |
| *Mie-mĭ* trebue, | ,, |
| I*mĭ* spune, | 'He tells me.' |
| I*mĭ* spune mie, | ,, |
| *Mie-mĭ* spune, | ,, |
| *Te rog dă-mi-l* mie, | 'I beseech thee to give it me.' |
| *Te rog dă-mi-l*, | ,,   ,, |
| *Dă mi-o*, | 'Give it me'(if the object is fem.). |
| *Dă-mi-o* mie, | ,, |

### THE REFLEXIVE PRONOUNS.

These are formed by adding to the personal pronouns the word *însu, însa*, 'self,' followed by the abbreviated dative of the corresponding person :

*Masculine.*

| | |
|---|---|
| E*ŭ* însu-*mĭ*, 'I myself.' | no*ĭ* înși-ne, |
| tu însu-*țĭ*, | vo*ĭ* înși-vĕ, |
| el însu-*șĭ*, | e*ĭ* înși-șĭ. |

*Feminine.*

| | |
|---|---|
| Eŭ însa-mĭ, | noĭ însi-ne, |
| tŭ însa-țĭ, | voĭ însi-vĕ, |
| ea însa-sĭ, | ele însi-le. |

*Note.*—For the third person, instead of the abbreviated form of *luĭ* or *eĭ*, we use another personal pronoun in the form *sĭ* for *sie*. This personal pronoun is made use of in genitive, dative, and accusative only :

Gen. *al sĕŭ*, ' his ;' dat. *sie*, ' to him ;' acc. *pe sine*, ' him.'

## Possessive Pronouns.

The possessive pronouns are as follows :—

| *meŭ*, | ' mine.' | *nostru*, | ' our.' |
|---|---|---|---|
| *tĕŭ*, | ' thine.' | *vostru*, | ' your.' |
| *sĕŭ* or *luĭ, eĭ*, ' his.' | | *lor* or *sĕĭ*, ' their.' |

They are treated as adjectives, agreeing in gender and number with the *object* of which they indicate the possession :

| *calul meŭ*, | ' my horse ;' | *caiĭ meĭ*, | ' my horses.' |
|---|---|---|---|
| *cassa mea*, | ' my house ;' | *cassele mele*, | ' my houses.' |

When they precede the noun (which they can do only in nominative and accusative), the article *al* for masculine, and *a* for feminine, and *aĭ*, *ale* for plural, are placed before them :

| *al meŭ căne*, | ' my dog ;' | *aĭ meĭ cănĭ*. |
|---|---|---|
| *a mea cassă*, | ' my house ;' | *a* or *ale mele casse*. |

## *Dumneat*a, *Dumneavóstră*.

In conversation it is usual, instead of using the direct personal pronoun *tu*, 'thou,' *voĭ*, 'you,' to use the compound words *dumneat*a, *dumneavóstră*, derived from *domnia ta*, 'thy lordship,' *domnia vóstră*, 'your lordship.'

These words have thus become a sort of personal pronoun. *Dumneavóstră* is also used for the singular as well as for the plural:

*Ce faceţĭ Dumneavóstră domnule*, 'How are you, sir?'

### Demonstrative Pronouns.

There are two demonstrative pronouns:

*acest, acéstă*, 'this' (for objects which are near).
*acel, acea*, 'that' (for objects which are further off).

They follow the rule of adjectives in agreeing with the nouns they indicate, in gender, number, and case. It is to be observed that *a* is the definite article for the masculine *acest, acel*.

We frequently use the abbreviated forms of these demonstratives:

ăst, astă  }  for *acest*.           ăl, aia    }  for *acel*.
ist, iastă, }                         cel, ceea }

### Interrogative and Relative Pronouns.

We put them under the same head because they are identical in form:

*care*, 'which;'   *ce*, 'what;'   *cine*, 'who.'

*Care* alone is declinable. *Cine* has only genitive and dative, *a cuĭ, cuĭ*.

## Indeterminate Pronouns.

Their list is very long, but it may be sufficient to indicate the principle of their formation, which is to prefix to the interrogative pronouns one of the particles *ori̯, veri̯, fie*:

orĭ cine,    orĭ care,    orĭ ce,  
verĭ cine,   verĭ care,   verĭ ce,  } whoever, whatever.  
fie cine,    fie care,    fie ce,

Or, by affixing the particle *va* to them:

cineva, careva, 'some one;' ceva, 'something.'

To these we add:

un, vre un, 'some one;' nici un, 'no one;'  
nimeni̯ or nime, 'nobody;'  
niște, 'some;' alt, 'other.'

---

## Verbs (Verbe).

In order to render the study of the verbs easier, we will class them under three heads, according to the termination of the infinitive present in *a*, *e*, or *i*. Before considering these inflections let us look at the three verbs—*a ave*, 'to have;' *a fi*, 'to be;' and *a voi*, 'to will;' which serve as auxiliary verbs. 'To will' being a regular verb, we insert it here only in the present indicative.

*A ave*, 'to have.'

*Indicative Present (Presentul Indicativuluĭ).*

eŭ am, 'I have.'        noĭ avem,  
tu aĭ,                  voĭ aveți,  
el are,                 eĭ aŭ.

When used as an auxiliary, an abbreviated form is given to the third person singular, and to the first and second persons plural. Thus—

eŭ am arat, 'I have ploughed.'    |   noĭ am arat (not avem arat).
tu aĭ arat,    |   voĭ aţĭ arat (not aveţĭ arat).
el or ea a arat (not are arat).    |   eĭ aŭ arat.

### Imperfect (Imperfect).

eŭ avém, 'I had' (j'avais).    |   noĭ avém,
tu avéĭ,    |   voĭ avéţĭ,
el avea,    |   eĭ avéŭ.

### Simple Perfect (Perfectul Simplu).

eŭ avuĭ, 'I had' (j'eus).    |   noĭ avurăm,
tu avuşĭ,    |   voĭ avurăţĭ,
el avu,    |   eĭ avură.

### Simple Pluperfect (Plusquam Perfectul Simplu).

eŭ avussem, 'I had had.'    |   noĭ avussem,
tu avussesĭ,    |   voĭ avusseţĭ,
el avusse,    |   eĭ avusse.

### Perfect (Perfect).

eŭ am avut, 'I have had.'    |   noĭ am avut,
tu aĭ avut,    |   voĭ aţĭ avut,
el a avut,    |   eĭ aŭ avut.

### Pluperfect (Plusquam Perfect).

eŭ am fost avut, 'I had had.'    |   noĭ am fost avut,
tu aĭ fost avut,    |   voĭ aţĭ fost avut,
el a fost avut,    |   eĭ aŭ fost avut.

### I. Future (*Viitorul întâi*).

eŭ voiŭ ave, 'I shall have.'  
tu veĭ aveĭ  
el va ave,

noĭ vom ave,  
voĭ veţĭ ave,  
eĭ vor ave.

### II. Future (*Viitorul al doilea*).

eŭ voiŭ fi avut, 'I shall have had.'  
tu veĭ fi avut,  
el va fi avut,

noĭ vom fi avut,  
voĭ veţĭ fi avut,  
eĭ vor fi avut.

### Imperative (*Imperativ*).

aibĭ (tu), 'Have.'  
aibe (el),

aveţĭ (voĭ),  
aibe (eĭ).

### Subjunctive Present (*Conjunctivul Present*).

eŭ să am, 'I may have.'  
tu să aĭ,  
el să aibă,

noĭ să avem,  
voĭ să aveţĭ,  
eĭ să aibă.

### Subjunctive Past (*Conjunctivul Trecut*).

eŭ să fi avut, 'I may have had.'  
tu să fi avut,  
el să fi avut,

noĭ să fi avut,  
voĭ să fi avut,  
eĭ să fi avut.

A subjunctive form of the future is frequently used instead of the indicative future:

o să am, 'I shall have.'  
o să aĭ,  
o să aibă,

o să avem,  
o să aveţĭ,  
o să aibă.

## Conditional Present (Conditional Pre3ent).

eŭ așĭ ave, 'I should have.'  
tu aĭ ave,  
el ar ave,

noĭ am ave,  
voĭ aṭĭ ave,  
eĭ ar ave.

## Conditional Past (Condițional Trecut).

eŭ așĭ fi avut, 'I should have [had.'  
tu aĭ fi avut,  
el ar fi avut,

noĭ am fi avut,  
voĭ aṭĭ fi avut,  
eĭ ar fi avut.

## Infinitive (Infinitiv).

Present.  
a ave, 'to have.'

Past (Trecut).  
a fi avut, 'to have had.'

## Participle (Particip).

Present.  
avĕnd, 'having.'

Past (Trecut).  
avut, 'had.'

---

## A fi, 'to be.'

### Indicative Present.

eŭ sunt, 'I am.'  
tu eșṭĭ,  
el este or e,

noĭ suntem,  
voĭ sunteṭĭ,  
eĭ sunt.

### Imperfect.

eŭ eram, 'I was' (j'étais).  
tu eraĭ,  
el era,

noĭ eram,  
voĭ eraṭĭ,  
eĭ eraŭ.

### Simple Perfect.

eŭ fuĭ, 'I was' (je fus).  |  noĭ furăm,
tu fuşĭ,                   |  voĭ furăţĭ,
el fu,                     |  eĭ fură.

### Simple Pluperfect.

eŭ fussem or fussessem, 'I had  |  noĭ fussessem,
tu fusseşĭ or fussesseşĭ, [been.'] |  voĭ fusseseţĭ,
el fusse or fussesse,           |  eĭ fussesse.

### Perfect.

eŭ am fost, 'I have been.'  |  noĭ am fost,
tu aĭ fost,                 |  voĭ aţĭ fost,
el a fost,                  |  eĭ aŭ fost.

### Pluperfect.

eŭ am fost fost, 'I had been.'  |  noĭ am fost fost,
tu aĭ   ,,                      |  voĭ aţĭ   ,,
el a    ,,                      |  eĭ aŭ    ,,

### I. Future.

eŭ voiŭ fi, 'I shall be.'  |  noĭ rom fi,
tu veĭ fi,                 |  voĭ veţĭ fi,
el va fi,                  |  eĭ vor fi.

### II. Future.

eŭ voiŭ fi fost, 'I shall have  |  noĭ vom fi fost,
tu veĭ   ,,         [been.']    |  voĭ veţĭ   ,,
el va    ,,                     |  eĭ vor    ,,

*Imperative.*

fiĭ (tu), 'Be.'　　　　　　　fiţĭ (voĭ),
fie (el),　　　　　　　　　　fie (eĭ).

*Subjunctive Present.*

eŭ să fiŭ, (If) 'I were.'　　noĭ să fim,
tu să fiĭ,　　　　　　　　　voĭ să fiţĭ,
el să fie,　　　　　　　　　eĭ să fie.

*Subjunctive Past.*

eŭ să fi fost, 'I may have been.'　noĭ să fi fost,
tu　,,　,,　　　　　　　　　　　voĭ　,,　,,
el　,,　,,　　　　　　　　　　　eĭ　,,　,,

*Subjunctive Future.*

eŭ o să fiŭ, 'Should I be.'　noĭ o să fim,
tu o să fiĭ,　　　　　　　　 voĭ o să fiţĭ,
el o să fie,　　　　　　　　 eĭ o să fie.

*Conditional Present.*

eŭ aşĭ fi, 'I should be.'　　noĭ am fi,
tu aĭ fi,　　　　　　　　　　voĭ aţĭ fi,
el ar fi,　　　　　　　　　　eĭ ar fi.

*Conditional Past.*

eŭ aşĭ fi fost, 'I should have　noĭ am fi fost,
tu aĭ　,,　　　　　[been.'　　voĭ aţĭ　,,
el ar　,,　　　　　　　　　　eĭ ar　,,

*Infinitive.*

| Present. | Past. |
|---|---|
| a fi, 'To be.' | a fi fost, 'To have been.' |

*Participle.*

| Present. | Past. |
|---|---|
| fiind, 'Being.' | fost, 'Been.' |

---

The same forms of the auxiliary verbs are used in the formation of the compound tenses, both of transitive and intransitive verbs. These forms are:—

1. Abbreviations of the indicative present of the verb 'to have,' for the perfect indicative:

| | |
|---|---|
| eŭ am arat, 'I have ploughed.' | noĭ am arat, |
| tu aĭ arat, | voĭ aţĭ arat, |
| el a arat, | eĭ aŭ arat. |

2. The same abbreviations with the past participle of the verb 'to be,' for the pluperfect indicative:

| | |
|---|---|
| eŭ am fost arat, 'I had ploughed.' | noĭ am fost arat, |
| tu aĭ fost arat, | voĭ aţĭ  ,, |
| el a  ,, ' | eĭ a  ,, |

3. The present indicative of the verb *a voi*, 'to will,' for the first future:

| | |
|---|---|
| eŭ voiŭ ara, 'I shall plough.' | noĭ vom ara, |
| tu veĭ ara, | voĭ veţĭ ara, |
| el va ara, | eĭ vor ara. |

4. The same present indicative, with the infinitive present of the verb 'to be,' for the second future:

| | | | | |
|---|---|---|---|---|
| eŭ voiŭ fi arat, | 'I shall have ploughed.' | | noĭ vom fi arat, | |
| tu veĭ | ,, | | voĭ veţĭ | ,, |
| el va | ,, | | eĭ vor | ,, |

5. As the subjunctive is formed by placing before the verb the particle să and the auxiliaries aşĭ, aĭ, ar, am, aţĭ, ar before the conditional, the perfects of those moods will be formed if we put after să or aşĭ the infinitive of 'to be:'

*Conditional Perfect.*

| | | | | |
|---|---|---|---|---|
| eŭ aşĭ fi arat, | 'I should have ploughed.' | | noĭ am fi arat, | |
| tu aĭ | ,, | | voĭ aţĭ | ,, |
| el ar | ,, | | eĭ ar | ,, |

*Subjunctive Perfect.*

| | | | | |
|---|---|---|---|---|
| eŭ să fi arat, | 'I may have ploughed.' | | noĭ să fi arat, | |
| tu | ,, | | voĭ | ,, |
| el | ,, | | eĭ | ,, |

And only in the passive form is the verb 'to be' used exclusively as auxiliary.

---

Having now considered the auxiliary verbs, and their use in the formation of the compound tenses of other verbs, we can speak of the verbs themselves. These have five different terminations for the infinitive present, which can be reduced to three.

Verbs ending in *a* long:

| | | | |
|---|---|---|---|
| *a a*ra, | 'to till.' | *a d*a, | 'to give.' |
| *a mă*nca, | 'to eat.' | *a l*ua, | 'to take;' etc. |

Verbs ending in *e* long, sometimes pronounced as the diphthong *ea*:

| | | | |
|---|---|---|---|
| *a av*e, | 'to have.' | *a ved*e, | 'to see.' |
| *a sed*e, | 'to sit.' | *a tăc*e, | 'to be silent;' etc. |

Verbs ending in *e* short:

| | | | |
|---|---|---|---|
| *a cred*e, | 'to believe.' | *a perd*e, | 'to lose.' |
| *a merg*e, | 'to go.' | *a aleg*e, | 'to choose, elect;' etc. |

The verbs ending in *e* long and in *e* short, as nearly similar in their inflections, may be classed together.

Verbs ending in *i* long:

| | | | |
|---|---|---|---|
| *a v*oi, | 'to will.' | *a iub*i, | 'to love.' |
| *a cinst*i, | 'to honour.' | *a opr*i, | 'to stop, to hinder;' etc. |

Verbs ending in *î* long (accentuated):

| | | | |
|---|---|---|---|
| *a omor*î, | 'to murder.' | *a ocăr*î, | 'to defame.' |
| *a cobor*î, | 'to descend.' | | etc. |

These two kinds may be classed together.

If we show the inflection of each of these three classes, and accompany them by such remarks as may be profitable, the student will form a complete idea of the Roumanian Verb.

## FIRST CLASS.

### A ara, 'to plough.'

*Indicative Present.*

| | |
|---|---|
| eŭ ar, 'I plough.' | noĭ arăm, |
| tu arĭ, | voĭ araṭĭ, |
| el ară, | eĭ ară. |

It is to be remarked that the third person singular of this class of verbs always ends in ă:—*el dă*, 'he gives;' *el mancă*, 'he eats;' *el spală*, 'he washes;' etc. The third person plural can end with *ă* or without it; thus—*eĭ ară* or *eĭ ar*, 'they till;' *eĭ spală* or *eĭ spăl*, 'they wash;' and when without *ă*, we prefer to add an *ŭ* (*mute*) to distinguish this plural from the first person singular, when they occur unaccompanied by pronouns:

| | | | |
|---|---|---|---|
| ar, | 'I plough;' | arŭ, | 'they plough.' |
| spăl, | 'I wash;' | spălŭ, | 'they wash.' |

etc.

But many verbs belonging to this class have a prolonged form in *ez* for the three persons singular and the third plural:

### a onora, 'to honour.'

| | |
|---|---|
| eŭ onorez, | noĭ onorăm, |
| tu onorezĭ, | voĭ onoraṭĭ, |
| el onoréză, | eĭ onoréză. |

So, too, *a respecta*, *a stima*, etc. These may take both forms, but there are others which can take only the form in *ez*, as *a vissa*, 'to dream,' *a lucra*, 'to work,' etc. This occurs also in the present subjunctive and imperative. It can be learnt only by practice.

### Imperfect.

eŭ aram, 'I ploughed' (je labourais).
tu araĭ,
el ara,

noĭ aram,
voĭ araţĭ,
eĭ araŭ or ara (in poetry).

### Simple Perfect.

eŭ araĭ, 'I ploughed' (je labourai).
tu araşĭ,
el ară,

noĭ ararăm,
voĭ ararăţĭ,
eĭ arară.

### Simple Pluperfect.

eŭ arassem, 'I had ploughed.'
tu arasseşĭ,
el arasse,

noĭ arassem,
voĭ arasseţĭ,
eĭ arasse.

These perfect and pluperfect tenses are frequently used in narration, whereas in conversation in speaking of past time the following compound perfect is used:

### Perfect.

eŭ am arat, 'I have ploughed.'
tu aĭ arat,
el a arat,

noĭ am arat,
voĭ aţĭ arat,
eĭ aŭ arat,

This perfect is used as frequently as the English imperfect, for expressing the time past.

### Pluperfect.

eŭ am fost arat, 'I had ploughed.'
tu aĭ ,, ,,
el a ,, ,,

noĭ am fost arat,
voĭ aţĭ ,, ,,
eĭ aŭ ,, ,,

Very little use is made of the pluperfect, or of the imperfect, unless in narration.

### I. *Future.*

| | |
|---|---|
| eŭ *voiŭ ara*, ' I shall plough.' | *noĭ vom ara,* |
| *tu veĭ ara,* | *voĭ veţĭ ara,* |
| *el va ara,* | *eĭ vor ara.* |

It may be remarked that *voiŭ*, the auxiliary for the future, is written with *ŭ* to distinguish it from the personal pronoun *voĭ*, ' you.'

### II. *Future.*

| | |
|---|---|
| eŭ *voiŭ fi arat,* ' I shall have ploughed.' | *noĭ vom fi arat,* |
| *tu veĭ* ,, | *voĭ veţĭ* ,, |
| *el va* ,, | *eĭ vor* ,, |

### *Imperative.*

| | |
|---|---|
| *ară (tu),* 'plough.' | *araţĭ (voĭ),* |
| *are (el),* | *are (eĭ).* |

### *Subjunctive Present.*

| | |
|---|---|
| eŭ *să ar,* ' I may plough.' | *noĭ să arăm,* |
| *tu să arĭ,* | *voĭ să araţĭ,* |
| *el să are,* | *eĭ să are.* |

It may be observed here that in the subjunctive the third person singular of verbs belonging to this class ends in *e*, whereas in those which have the infinitive in *e* and *i*, it ends in *ă*.

### *Subjunctive Past.*

| | |
|---|---|
| eŭ *să fi arat,* ' I may have ploughed.' | *noĭ să fi arat.* |
| *tu* ,, | *voĭ* ,, |
| *el* ,, | *eĭ* ,, |

Some use this subjunctive as follows :

  *eŭ să fiŭ arat,*      *noĭ să fim arat,*
  *tu să fiĭ arat,*      *voĭ să fiţĭ arat,*
  *el să fie arat,*      *eĭ să fie arat.*

But the former is more correct.

### I. Conditional.

*eŭ aşĭ ara,* 'I should plough.'    *noĭ am ara,*
*tu aĭ ara,*         *voĭ aţĭ ara,*
*el ar ara,*         *eĭ ar ara.*

### II. Conditional.

*eŭ aşĭ fi arat,* 'I should have ploughed.'    *noĭ am fi arat,*
*tu aĭ*  ,,        *voĭ aţĭ*  ,,
*el ar*  ,,        *eĭ ar*  ,,

### Infinitive.

*Present.*        *Past.*
*a ara* or *arare,* 'to plough.'    *a fi arat,* 'to have ploughed.'

### Participle.

*Present.*        *Past.*
*arănd,* 'ploughing.'      *arat,* 'ploughed.'

As seen here, the infinitive present has two forms. The first, as a verb, is preceded by the particle *a*, corresponding to the English 'to:' *a ara,* 'to plough,' *a da,* 'to give,' etc.; and the second form is treated as a noun : *arare, dare,* etc.

## SECOND CLASS.

a vede, 'to see.'        a crede, 'to believe.'

*Indicative Present.*

eŭ vĕd, 'I see.'         eŭ cred, 'I believe.'
tu vedĭ,                 tu credĭ,
el vede,                 el crede.
noĭ vedem,               noĭ credem,
voĭ vedeţĭ,              voĭ credeţĭ,
eĭ vĕd or vede.          eĭ cred or crede.

We see here that the third person singular of the verbs of the second class ends in *e*, whereas in the case of the first class it ends in *ă*. The third person plural is *vede*, *crede*, ending thus with *e*; but this plural is often without it, in which case, to distinguish this third person plural from the first singular, we add an *ŭ*:

vĕd,  'I see;'       rĕdŭ,  'they see.'
cred, 'I believe;'   credŭ, 'they believe.'
                etc.

With regard to the accent, we remark that in this tense and also in the subjunctive present, the verbs ending in *e* long have the accent on their final e*m*, e*ţĭ*, of the first and second persons plural, whereas those ending in *e* short have the accent on the previous syllable:

*ved*em,  'we see;'       vedeţĭ,  'you see;'
credem,   'we believe;'   credeţĭ, 'you believe;'

this being the only difference in their conjugation.

## Imperfect.

| | |
|---|---|
| eŭ vedém, 'I saw.' | eŭ credém, 'I believed.' |
| tu vedéĭ, | tu credéĭ, |
| el vedea, | el credea, |
| noĭ vedém, | noĭ credém, |
| voĭ vedéţĭ, | voĭ credéţĭ, |
| eĭ vedéŭ. | eĭ credéŭ. |

We know that é with the accent is equivalent to the diphthong ea, but as é for ea cannot be written at the end of a word, we have—

el credea (not credé).   el vedea (not vedé).

## Simple Perfect.

| | |
|---|---|
| eŭ vĕduĭ, 'je vis.' | eŭ creduĭ, |
| tu vĕduşĭ, | tu creduşĭ, |
| el vĕdu, | el credu, |
| noĭ vĕdurăm, | noĭ credurăm, |
| voĭ vĕdurăţĭ, | voĭ credurăţĭ, |
| eĭ vĕdură. | eĭ credură. |

There are many verbs ending in e short which instead of uĭ take eĭ for the simple perfect, and change the last consonant to s; so a merge, 'to go,' has not its simple perfect eŭ merguĭ, but—

| | |
|---|---|
| eŭ merseĭ, 'I went.' | noĭ merserăm, |
| tu merseşĭ, | voĭ merserăţĭ, |
| el merse, | eĭ merseră. |

Thus:

| | | | |
|---|---|---|---|
| a scrie, | 'to write;' | perfect, | eŭ scrisseĭ. |
| a duce, | 'to bring;' | ,, | eŭ dusseĭ. |

*a purcede,* ' to start ;'   perfect,   *eŭ purcesseĭ.*
*a alege,*   ' to choose ;'     ,,      *eŭ alesseĭ.*
*a culege,*  ' to gather ;'     ,,      *eŭ culesseĭ.*
    etc.

It will be shown that the past participle of these verbs is also different from the past participles of other verbs, and therefore all their compound tenses will differ too, as also the simple pluperfect, as it is formed from the simple perfect.

## Simple Pluperfect.

*eŭ vĕdussem,* ' I had seen.'  *eŭ credussem,* ' I had believed.'
*tu vĕdussesĭ.*      *tu credussesĭ.*
*el vĕdusse.*       *el credusse.*
*noĭ vĕdussem.*      *noĭ credussem.*
*oĭ vĕdusseţĭ.*      *voĭ credusseţĭ.*
*eĭ vĕdusse.*       *eĭ credusse.*

  *a scrie* will have, of course,   *eŭ scrissessem.*
  *a duce*  ,,  ,,  *eŭ dussessem.*
      etc.

## Perfect.

*eŭ am vĕdut,* ' I have seen.'  *eŭ am credut,* ' I have believed.'
*tu aĭ vĕdut,*       *tu aĭ credut.*
*el a vĕdut,*       *el a credut.*
*noĭ am vĕdut,*      *noĭ am credut.*
*voĭ aţĭ vĕdut,*      *voĭ aţĭ credut.*
*eĭ aŭ vĕdut,*       *eĭ aŭ credut.*

## Pluperfect.

eŭ am fost vĕdut, ' I had seen.'   eŭ am fost credut, 'I had believed.'
tu aĭ ,, ,,                        tu aĭ ,, ,,
el a ,, ,,                         el a ,, ,,
noĭ am ,, ,,                       noĭ am ,, ,,
voĭ aţĭ ,, ,,                      voĭ aţĭ ,, ,,
eĭ aŭ ,, ,,                        eĭ aŭ ,, ,,

As we remarked before, this tense is very rarely made use of.

### I. Future.

' I shall see.'           ' I shall believe.'
eŭ voiŭ vede,             eŭ voiŭ crede,
tu veĭ ,,                 tu veĭ ,,
el va ,,                  el va ,,
noĭ vom ,,                noĭ vom ,,
voĭ veţĭ ,,               voĭ veţĭ ,,
eĭ vor ,,                 eĭ vor ,,

### II. Future.

' I shall have seen.'     ' I shall have believed.'
eŭ voiŭ fi vĕdut,         eŭ voiŭ fi credut,
tu veĭ ,,                 tu veĭ ,,
el va ,,                  el va ,,
noĭ vom ,,                noĭ vom ,,
voĭ veţĭ ,,               voĭ veţĭ ,,
eĭ vor ,,                 eĭ vor ,,

### Imperative.

vedĭ (tu), ' see.'        crede (tu), ' believe.'
védă (el),                crédă (el),
vedeţĭ (voĭ),             credeţĭ (voĭ),
védă (eĭ).                crédă (eĭ).

I. *Subjunctive.*

| | |
|---|---|
| eŭ să vĕd, 'I may see.' | eŭ să cred, 'I may believe.' |
| tu să vedĭ, | tu să credĭ, |
| el să védă, | el să crédă, |
| noĭ să vedem, | noĭ să credem, |
| voĭ să vedeţĭ, | voĭ să credeţĭ, |
| eĭ să védă. | eĭ să crédĕ. |

We remark once more that the third person singular ends in *e* in the indicative for the verbs of the second and third classes, and in *ă* for the conjunctive; whereas for those of the first class, and for those ending in *i* long, the rule is inverted.

II. *Subjunctive.*

| | | | |
|---|---|---|---|
| eŭ să fi vĕdut, 'I may have seen.' | | eŭ să fi credut, 'I may have believed.' | |
| tu să | ,, | tu să | ,, |
| el să | ,, | el să | ,, |
| noĭ să | ,, | noĭ să | ,, |
| voĭ să | ,, | voĭ să | ,, |
| eĭ să | ,, | eĭ să | ,, |

I. *Conditional.*

| | | | |
|---|---|---|---|
| eŭ aşĭ vede, 'I should see.' | | eŭ aşĭ crede, 'I should believe.' | |
| tu aĭ | ,, | tu aĭ | ,, |
| el ar | ,, | el ar | ,, |
| noĭ am | ,, | noĭ am | ,, |
| voĭ aţĭ | ,, | voĭ aţĭ | ,, |
| eĭ ar | ,, | eĭ ar | ,, |

## II. *Conditional.*

| | | |
|---|---|---|
| eŭ așĭ fi vĕdut, 'I should have seen.' | | eŭ așĭ fi credut, 'I should have believed.' |
| tu aĭ     „ | | tu aĭ     „ |
| el ar     „ | | el ar     „ |
| noĭ am fi vĕdut, | | noĭ am fi credut, |
| voĭ ațĭ   „ | | voĭ ațĭ   „ |
| eĭ ar     „ | | eĭ ar     „ |

### *Infinitive.*

| *Present.* | *Past.* |
|---|---|
| a vede or vedere, 'to see.' | a fi vĕdut, 'to have seen.' |
| a crede, credere, 'to believe.' | a fi credut 'to have believed.' |

It is well to note the accented syllable of the second form of the infinitive present. As we said before, this second form is used as a noun. Its intonation depends on the former infinitive, from which it is derived.

### *Participles.*

| *Present.* | *Past.* |
|---|---|
| vĕdĕnd, 'seeing.' | vĕdut, 'seen.' |
| credĕnd, 'believing.' | credut, 'believed.' |

As we remarked before, the past participle of some verbs belonging to this class will not end in *ut*, but will consist of the root with the final consonant changed to *s*:

| | | | |
|---|---|---|---|
| a merge, | 'to go;' | past participle, | mers, |
| a duce, | 'to bring;' | „ | dus, |
| a pune, | 'to put;' | „ | pus. |

etc.

The simple perfect is made by adding *eĭ* to the past participle.

## THIRD CLASS.

*a dorm*i, ' to sleep ;'   *a omorî*, ' to murder.'

### Indicative Present.

| | |
|---|---|
| eŭ *dorm*, ' I sleep.' | eŭ *omor*, ' I murder.' |
| tu *dorm*ĭ, | tu *omor*ĭ, |
| el *dórme*, | el *omóră*, |
| noĭ *dorm*im, | noĭ *omor*îm, |
| voĭ *dorm*iţĭ, | voĭ *omor*îţĭ, |
| eĭ *dorm*, or | |
| eĭ *dórme*, (in verse,) | eĭ *omor* or *omóră*. |

Many verbs have a prolonged form in *esc* for the three persons singular and the third plural :

*a iub*i, ' to love ;'   *a pîrî*, ' to speak ill.'

| | |
|---|---|
| eŭ *iubesc*, ' I love.' | eŭ *pîrĕsc*, ' I speak ill.' |
| tu *iubeştĭ*, | tu *pîrĕştĭ*, |
| el *iubeşte*, | el *pîreşte*, |
| noĭ *iub*im, | noĭ *pîr*îm, |
| voĭ *iub*iţĭ, | voĭ *pîr*îţĭ, |
| eĭ *iubesc*, | eĭ *pîrĕsc*. |

The same occurs in the present conjunctive and imperative.

### Imperfect.

| | |
|---|---|
| eŭ *dormiam*, ' I slept.' | eŭ *omoriam*, ' I murdered.' |
| tu *dormiaĭ*, | tu *omoriaĭ*, |
| el *dormia*, | el *omoria*, |
| noĭ *dormiam*, | noĭ *omoriam*, |
| voĭ *dormiaţĭ*, | voĭ *omoriaţĭ*. |
| eĭ *dormiaŭ* | eĭ *omoriaŭ*. |

## Simple Perfect.

eŭ dormiĭ, 'I slept.'  
tu dormiṣĭ,  
el dormi,  
noĭ dormirăm,  
voĭ dormirățĭ,  
eĭ dormiră,

eŭ omorîĭ, 'I murdered.'  
tu omorîşĭ,  
el omorî,  
noĭ omorîrăm,  
voĭ omorîrățĭ,  
eĭ omorîră.

## Simple Pluperfect.

eŭ dormissem, 'I had slept.'  
tu dormisseşĭ,  
el dormisse,  
noĭ dormissem,  
voĭ dormisseţĭ,  
eĭ dormisse,

eŭ omorîssem, 'I had murdered.'  
tu omorîsseşĭ,  
el omorîsse,  
noĭ omorîssem,  
voĭ omorîsseţĭ,  
eĭ omorîsse.

## Perfect.

eŭ am dormit, 'I have slept.'  
tu aĭ dormit,  
el a dormit,  
noĭ am dormit,  
voĭ aţĭ dormit,  
eĭ aŭ dormit,

eŭ am omorît, 'I have murdered.'  
tu aĭ omorît,  
el a omorît,  
noĭ am omorît,  
voĭ aţĭ omorît,  
eĭ aŭ omorît.

## Pluperfect.

eŭ am fost dormit, 'I had slept.'  
tu aĭ fost dormit,  
el a fost dormit,

eŭ am fost omorît, 'I had murdered.'  
tu aĭ fost omorît,  
el a fost omorît,

noĭ am fost dormit,  noĭ am fost omorît,
voĭ aṭĭ fost dormit,  voĭ aṭĭ fost omorît,
eĭ aŭ fost dormit,  eĭ aŭ fost omorît.

We repeat once more, in order to impress upon the student's mind that we very rarely make use of this pluperfect, that we generally employ the perfect—eŭ am arat, eŭ am vĕdut, eŭ am credut, etc.—to express the past time (as in English the imperfect), and that the perfect and pluperfect simple are used more in narration.

### I. Future.

| | | | | | |
|---|---|---|---|---|---|
| eŭ voiŭ dormi, | 'I shall sleep.' | | eŭ voiŭ omorî, | 'I shall murder.' | |
| tu veĭ | ,, | | tu veĭ | ,, | |
| el va | ,, | | el va | ,, | |
| noĭ vom | ,, | | noĭ vom | ,, | |
| voĭ veṭĭ | ,, | | voĭ veṭĭ | ,, | |
| eĭ vor | ,, | | eĭ vor | ,, | |

### II. Future.

| | | | | | |
|---|---|---|---|---|---|
| eŭ voiŭ fi dormit, | 'I shall have slept.' | | eŭ voiŭ fi omorît, | 'I shall have murdered.' | |
| tu veĭ | ,, | | tu veĭ | ,, | |
| el va | ,, | | el va | ,, | |
| noĭ vom | ,, | | noĭ vom | ,, | |
| voĭ veṭĭ | ,, | | voĭ veṭĭ | ,, | |
| eĭ vor | ,, | | eĭ vor | ,, | |

### Imperative.

dormĭ (tu), 'sleep.'  omóră (tu), 'murder.'
dórmă (el),  omóre (el),
dormiṭĭ (voĭ),  omoriṭĭ (voĭ),
dórmă (eĭ),  omóre (eĭ).

Here, as well as in the indicative present and subjunctive present, the verbs ending in *î* differ a little from those ending in *i* in the second person singular, and in the third persons singular and plural.

*Subjunctive Present.*

eŭ să dorm, 'I may sleep.'  
tu să dormĭ,  
el să dórmă,  
noĭ să dormim,  
voĭ să dormiţĭ,  
eĭ să dórmă,

eŭ să omor, 'I may murder.'  
tu să omorĭ,  
el să omóre,  
noĭ să omorîm,  
voĭ să omorîţĭ,  
eĭ să omóre.

II. *Subjunctive.*

eŭ să fi dormit, 'I may have slept.'  
tu ,, ,,  
el ,, ,,  
noĭ ,, ,,  
voĭ ,, ,,  
eĭ ,, ,,

eŭ să fi omorît, 'I may have murdered.'  
tu ,, ,,  
el ,, ,,  
noĭ ,, ,,  
voĭ ,, ,,  
eĭ ,, ,,

I. *Conditional.*

eŭ aşĭ dormi, 'I should sleep.'  
tu aĭ ,,  
el ar ,,  
noĭ am ,,  
voĭ aţĭ ,,  
eĭ ar ,,

eŭ aşĭ omorî, 'I should murder.'  
tu aĭ ,,  
el ar ,,  
noĭ am ,,  
voĭ aţĭ ,,  
eĭ ar ,,

## II. *Conditional.*

| | | |
|---|---|---|
| eŭ așĭ fi dormit, | 'I should have slept.' | eŭ așĭ fi omorît, 'I should have murdered.' |
| tu aĭ fi dormit, | | tu aĭ fi omorît, |
| el ar ,, ,, | | el ar ,, ,, |
| noĭ am ,, ,, | | noĭ am ,, ,, |
| voĭ aṭĭ ,, ,, | | voĭ aṭĭ ,, ,, |
| eĭ ar ,, ,, | | eĭ ar ,, ,, |

### *Infinitive.*

| *Present.* | *Past.* |
|---|---|
| a dormi or dormire, 'to sleep.' | a fi dormit, 'to have slept.' |
| a omorî or omorîre, 'to murder.' | a fi omorît, 'to have murdered.' |

### *Participle.*

| *Present.* | *Past.* |
|---|---|
| dormind, 'sleeping.' | dormit, 'slept.' |
| omorînd, 'murdering.' | omorît, 'murdered.' |

## THE ACCENT OF VERBS.

It was observed, with regard to the nouns and adjectives, that the accented syllable remains still accented whatever be the number of syllables added to them; thus, om, omuluĭ, ómenilor, etc. The only exception to it is when we affix diminutive or augmentative suffixes to a noun, in which case the accent falls upon those suffixes.

With regard to the verbs, the intonation rests upon the suffix :--

eŭ ar, eŭ aram, eŭ araĭ, etc.

If the suffix consists of more than one syllable, the accent is upon the first syllable of the suffix :

ararăm, arassem, etc.

Exceptions are :

(1) The verbs ending in *e* short, in the first and second persons plural of the indicative present and subjunctive present, and in the plural of the imperative :—

*credem, credețĭ; să credem, să credețĭ; credețĭ (voĭ), crédă (eĭ).*

(2) The third persons singular and plural of the indicative present, subjunctive present, and imperative of all verbs :—

*el ară, el vede, el dórme*, etc.

## The Passive Voice.

For the passive voice we use the auxiliary verb *a fi*, 'to be,' by adding to each tense of this auxiliary the past participle of the verb we require. In this case the participle, being considered more as an adjective than as a verb, will agree with its subject in gender as well as in number.

*A fi iubit*, 'To be loved.'

| | | | |
|---|---|---|---|
| Indicative present, | *Sunt iubit, iubită,* | *suntem iubițĭ, iubite,* | |
| Imperfect . . . | *Eram* ,, ,, | *eramŭ* ,, ,, . | |
| Perfect. . . . | *Am fost* ,, ,, | ,, ,, ,, | |
| | etc. | | |

## The Reflexive Form.

This form belongs to verbs the subject and object of which are identical. The pronoun indicating the object is placed before the verb in the dative or accusative case, as the verb may require, and in its abbreviated form:—

*With Accusative.*  *With Dative.*

se mira, 'to be astonished.' | a și propune, 'to propose to oneself.'

*Indicative Present.*

eŭ mĕ mir, 'I am astonished.'   eŭ îmĭ propun, 'I propose to
tu te mirĭ,                     tu ĭțĭ propuĭ,           [myself.'
el se miră,                     el îșĭ propune,
noĭ ne mirăm,                   noĭ ne propunem,
voĭ vĕ miraţĭ,                  voĭ vĕ propuneţĭ,
eĭ se miră,                     eĭ îșĭ propun.

*Imperfect.*

eŭ mĕ miram,              eŭ îmĭ propuném,
'I was astonished.'       'I proposed to myself.'

*Simple Perfect.*

eŭ mĕ miraĭ,              eŭ îmĭ propusseĭ.
'I was astonished.'       'I proposed to myself.'

*Simple Pluperfect.*

eŭ mĕ mirassem,           eŭ îmĭ propussessem.
'I had been astonished.'  'I had proposed to myself.'

## Perfect.

eŭ m'am mĭrat, 'I have been astonished.'  
tu te-aĭ mirat,  
el s'a „  
noĭ ne-am „  
voĭ v'aţĭ „  
eĭ s'aŭ „  

eŭ mi-am propus, 'I have proposed to myself.'  
tu ţi-aĭ propus,  
el şi-a „  
noĭ ne-am „  
voĭ v'aţĭ „  
eĭ şi-aŭ „  

## Pluperfect.

eŭ m'am fost mirat.  
'I had been astonished.'

eŭ mi-am fost propus.  
'I had proposed to myself.'

### I. Future.

cŭ mĕ voiŭ mira,  
'I shall be astonished.'

eŭ îmĭ voiŭ propune.  
'I shall propose to myself.'

### II. Future.

eŭ mĕ voiŭ fi mirat,  
'I shall have been astonished.'

eŭ îmĭ voiŭ fi propus.  
'I shall have proposed to myself.'

## Imperative.

miră-te, 'be astonished.'  
mire-se,  
miraţi-vĕ,  
mire-se,  

propune-ţĭ, 'propose to thyself.'  
propunĕ-şĭ,  
propuneţi-vĕ,  
propunĕ-şĭ.  

### I. Subjunctive.

eŭ să mĕ mir,  
'I may be astonished.'

eŭ să-mĭ propun,  
'I may propose to myself.'

## II. Subjunctive.

eŭ să me fi mirat,       eŭ să-mĭ fi propus,
'I may have been astonished.'    'I may have proposed to myself.'

### I. Conditional.

| | | | |
|---|---|---|---|
| eŭ m'aşĭ mira, 'I should be astonished.' | | eŭ mi-aşĭ propune, 'I should propose to myself.' | |
| tu te-aĭ mira | | tu ţi-aĭ propune | |
| el s'ar | ,, | el şi-ar | ,, |
| noĭ ne-am | ,, | noĭ ne-am | ,, |
| voĭ v'aţĭ | ,, | voĭ v'aţĭ | ,, |
| eĭ s'ar | ,, | eĭ şi-ar | ,, |

### II. Conditional.

eŭ m'aşĭ fi mirat,      eŭ mi-aşĭ fi propus.
'I should have been astonished.'    'I should have proposed to myself.'

### Infinitive.

| Present. | Perfect. |
|---|---|
| a se mira, 'to be astonished.' | a se fi mirat, 'to have been astonished.' |
| a-şĭ propune, 'to propose to oneself.' | o-şĭ fi propus. 'to have proposed to oneself.' |

### Participle.

mirănd-u-se,      propunĕnd-u-şĭ.
'being astonished.'    'proposing to oneself.'

It will be observed that in the imperative and present participle the pronouns follow the verb.

## IRREGULAR VERBS.

The study of the verbs in Roumanian is the easier for the fact that there is not a long list of what are called anomalous verbs, as in German or in French. Besides the verbs *a ave*, *a fi*, the conjugation of which we have already seen, the following verbs must be noticed:

(1) *A şti*, 'to know,' which though belonging to the third class (according to its final *i*) is inflected as one of the second class:

  eŭ ştiŭ,  eŭ ştiuĭ,  eŭ ştiussem.
  'I know,'  'I knew,'  'I had known.'

(2) *A voi*, 'to will,' which though regularly inflected may take the following alternative form in all its tenses:

### Indicative Present.

  eŭ voesc, 'I will.'  eŭ vreŭ,
  tu voeştĭ,  tu vreĭ,
  el voeste,  el vre, or vrea,
  noĭ voim,  noĭ vrem,
  voĭ voiţĭ,  voĭ vreţĭ,
  eĭ voescŭ,  eĭ·vreŭ, or vréŭ.

### Imperfect.

eŭ voiam, 'I was willing.'  eŭ vrém,

### Simple Perfect.

eŭ voiĭ, 'I was willing.'  eŭ vrusseĭ.

### Simple Pluperfect.

eŭ voissem, 'I had been willing.'  eŭ vrussem.

## VERBS.

### Perfect.

eŭ am voit, 'I have been willing.'  eŭ am vrut.

### Pluperfect.

eŭ am fost voit, 'I had been willing.'  eŭ am fost vrut.

### I. Future.

eŭ voiŭ voi, 'I shall be willing.'  eŭ voiŭ vre.

### II. Future.

eŭ voiŭ fi voit, 'I shall have been willing.'  eŭ voiŭ fi vrut.

### Imperative.

voește (tu), 'be willing.'  vrea (tu),
voéscă (el),  vree (el),
voiți (voĭ),  vretĭ (voĭ),
voéscă (eĭ),  vree (eĭ).

### I. Subjunctive.

eŭ să voesc, 'I may be willing.'  eŭ să vreŭ.

### II. Subjunctive.

eŭ să fi voit, 'I may have been willing.'  eŭ să fi vrut,

### I. Conditional.

eŭ așĭ voi,  'I should be willing.'  eŭ așĭ vre,

### II. Conditional.

eŭ așĭ fi voit, 'I should have been willing.'  eŭ așĭ fi vrut.

### Infinitive.

Present.  Perfect.

a voi, 'to be willing,' a vre. | a fi voit, 'to have been willing,'
a fi vrut.

Both forms are correct, but the first is more acceptable.

(3) *A lu*a, 'to take,' has a regular conjugation, but in the singular, and the third person plural of the indicative present, subjunctive present, and imperative, it changes the root *lu* to *i*.

*Indicative Present.*

eŭ *ia*ŭ, 'I take.'   noĭ *lu*ăm,
tu *ia*ĭ,            voĭ *lu*aţĭ.
el *i*a,             eĭ *ia*ŭ.

*Imperative.*

*i*a (*tu*), 'take.'   *lu*aţĭ (*vo*ĭ),
*i*a (*el*),           *i*a (*e*ĭ).

*Subjunctive Present.*

eŭ să *ia*ŭ, 'I may take.'   noĭ să *lu*ăm,
tu să *ia*ĭ,                 voĭ să *lu*aţĭ,
el să *i*a,                  eĭ să *i*a.

(4) Many verbs derived from those Latin verbs which reduplicate their root for the perfect do the same in Roumanian:

*a da*, 'to give;' eŭ *dădu*ĭ; participle *dat*.
*a sta*, 'to stay;' eŭ *stătu*ĭ;   „   *stat*.

In the same way, *a la*, 'to wash (the head),' has its perfect:

eŭ *lău*ĭ, past participle *lăut* or *lat*.

(5) The verbs, *a zice*, 'to say;' *a face*, 'to do,' have the second person singular of the imperative: *zi*, *fă*.

## IMPERSONAL VERBS.

The impersonal verbs, *a plo*u*a*, 'to rain;' *a ninge*, 'to snow;' *a du*r*e*, 'to feel pain,' are conjugated regularly.

---

## Adverbs (Adverbe).

(1.) Some adjectives in the masculine gender serve as adverbs: *căntă frumos*, 'he (or she) sings beautifully.'

In some of the adverbs we can trace the principle of their formation. For instance, adjectives ending in *esc*, change this termination to *eşte* to form adverbs:

*dom*n*esc*, 'princely;' *domneşte*, 'princely.'
*bărbătesc*, 'manly;' *bărbăteşte*, 'manly.'
*ăngeresc*, 'angelical;' *ăngereşte*, 'angelically.'

These adverbs, like the adjectives from which they are derived, express for the most part manner or qualification. But there are other adverbs indicating quantity, time, place, affirmation, negation, doubt, of which we give a list, as their number is limited, and they are very frequently used.

(2.) *Adverbs of Quantity.*

*ma*ĭ, more.
încă, (encore), further, still, more.
*numa*ĭ, solely, only.

(3.) *Adverbs of Place.*

*un*d*e*, where.
*ac*i, here.
*acol*o, there.

*d*incolo, the other side.
*d*incóce, this side.
*afară*, without, except, out.

*înuntru*, in.
*d'assupra*, above.
*de desubt*, below.
*dindărăt*, behind.
*dinainte*, before.
*d'alăturĭ*, near, by.
*faţă*, present.
*pretutindenĭ*, everywhere.
*orĭ unde*, everywhere.

*nicăĭrĭ*, nowhere.
*undeva*, somewhere.
*óre unde*, somewhere.
*aiure*, elsewhere.
*aprópe*, near.
*departe*, far.
*d'a drépta*, on the right.
*d'a stînga*, on the left.

(4.) *Adverbs of Time.*

*cînd*, when.
*acum*, now.
*acuşĭ*, presently.
*îndată*, instantly.
*azĭ*, to-day.
*mînĭ*, to-morrow.
*erĭ* (*e* read as *ye* in 'yes'), yesterday.
*dĕunăzĭ*, the other day.
*demult*, long ago.
*cîte o dată*, sometimes.

*une orĭ*, sometimes.
*orĭ cînd*, whenever.
*óre cînd*, once.
*timpuriŭ*, early.
*tărziŭ*, late.
*adesse*, often.
*nicĭ o dată*, never.
*pe urmă*, then, next to.
*curînd*, shortly.
*atuncĭ*, then.
*după ce*, after.

(5.) *Adverbs of Affirmation.*

*da*, yes.
*aşa*, so.
*adevărat*, verily, truly.
*fără indoială*, doubtless.
*negreşit*, of course.

*sigur*, certainly.
*zeŭ*, by God (abbreviated from *Dumnezeŭ*, 'God').
*iată*, lo! behold.

## (6.) *Negative Adverbs.*

*n*u, no.
*nu a*ș*a,* not so.
*ni*m*ic,* nothing.

*nic*ĭ *cum,* not at all.
*ba,* } no.
*ba nu,* }

## (7) *Adverbs expressing a doubt.*

*dór,* }
*póte,* } perhaps.
*óre,* }

*cam* ( *à peu près*), nearly, about.

## Prepositions.

These are particles the origin of which is very difficult to find out, and it will be sufficient to give a list of them:

*a,* at, (à).
*de a,* } from.
*de la,* }
*la,* at.
*pe,* upon.
*de,* by.
*din,* from.

*fără,* without.
*in,* in.
*pentru,* for.
*spre,* towards.
*pănă,* till.
*după,* after, according to.
*contra,* against.

These are independent particles, but there are some which are prefixed to words, modifying their meaning, or giving them more force:

*des, es, e, con, pre, stră.*

EXAMPLES:—*taină,* ' mystery ; ' *destăinuesc,* ' divulge ; ' *mo*ș, ' uncle ;' *strămo*ș, ' ancestor,' etc.

## Conjunctions.

These particles are of different kinds. The most usual are as follows:

și, and.
iar, } but.
însă, }
dacă, } if.
de, }
deci, then, (donc).
că, that.
dar, but.
prin urmare, consequently.

căci, } because.
pentru că }
adecă, to wit.
precum, as.
ci, but.
totuși, still.
numai, but.
de vreme ce, } since.
de óre ce, }

## Interjections.

These are the most usual interjections:

a! ah.
vai! woe!
aleŭ, alas!

hei, ho.
bre, (admiration).

# SYNTAX.

WE propose to show here very briefly how to combine the different parts and particles of speech, in order to make a correct Roumanian sentence.

## THE NOUNS.

### NOMINATIVE.

The subject of the verb is put in the nominative case, and its place is at the beginning of the sentence:

*Trandafirul este o flóre frumóssă,* 'The rose is a pretty flower;'
*Dumnezeŭ a zidit lumea,* 'God has created the world.'

### GENITIVE.

The dependence of one noun upon another is indicated by the genitive case:

*Flórea cîmpuluĭ,* 'The flower of the field;'
*Cartea copiluluĭ,* 'The book of the child.'

We see here that when the genitive follows the subject, the particle *a* is omitted. But when the genitive precedes the subject, as it often does in verse, the particle *a* cannot be omitted. In such case the subject is without the article:

*a cîmpuluĭ flóre,* 'the field's flower;'
*a copiluluĭ carte,* 'the child's book.'

## Dative.

The case governed indirectly by the verb, follows the case governed directly:

*Am dat cartea copiluluĭ,* 'I gave the book to the child.'

We have however already seen that the genitive, when it follows a noun, loses its particle *a*. When in such a sentence as the above it would not at first sight be obvious whether by the expression *cartea copiluluĭ* was meant 'the book of the child' or 'the book to the child,' the confusion which might then arise is avoided by placing the dative next to the verb:

*am dat copiluluĭ cartea.*

## Accusative.

When the direct object of a transitive verb is a person, it takes the accusative case preceded by the preposition *pe*; in all other cases the accusative without that preposition is used:

*Copilul bun stiméză pe părinţĭ,* 'The good child honours the parents.'

*Am vĕdut palatul Regal,* 'I have seen the Royal palace.'

When a noun in the accusative case is followed by an adjective or a possessive pronoun, it takes the article:

*Copilul bun stiméză pe părinţiĭ sĕĭ,* 'The good child honours his parents.'

## Vocative.

We have already seen that the vocative singular of masculine nouns ends in *e*, and that of feminine nouns in *o*, the plural of both being in *lor*.

## SYNTAX.

For the masculine singular the nouns generally preserve their article in the vocative:

  *Omule!* 'O man!'  *Dumnezeule!* 'O God!'

The article, however, is very often suppressed:

| | | | |
|---|---|---|---|
| *O dómne,* | 'O Lord,' | instead of | *O domnule.* |
| *O împărate,* | 'O Emperor,' | ,, | ,, *O împăratule.* |
| *O amice,* | 'O friend,' | ,, | ,, *O amicule.* |

     etc.

But when the noun in the vocative case is connected with other words, we use, instead of the vocative, the nominative with the article—sometimes, but not always, preceded by *O*:

  *O amicul meŭ,*  'O my friend.'
  *O sora mea,*   'O my sister.'
     etc.

### ABLATIVE.

The ablative case is preceded by one of the particles, *în, de, la,* etc.

The dependence of one noun upon another, usually expressed by a genitive, can also be indicated by an ablative with *de*:

  *Flórea cîmpuluĭ,*
  *Flóre de cîmp,*  } 'The flower of the field.'

This is necessary when the attribute expresses the substance or the purpose of the noun to which it refers:

  *Minte de copil,*  'Childish mind.'
  *Palat de crystal,*  'Crystal palace.'
  *Picior de lemn,*  'Wooden leg.'
  *Carte de cetit,*  'Book to be read.'

In the case of verbs governing two objects, the ablative case with *de* may be used, instead of the accusative, to indicate one of those objects:

*Statul l'a ales president*, or *Statul l'a ales de president*,
'The State elected him as President.'

## ADJECTIVES.

We have already seen in studying the etymology that these can either precede or follow the nouns to which they refer, while always agreeing with them in gender and number.

## PRONOUNS.

The order of the words in a sentence is generally as follows—subject, verb, object:

*Am vĕdut pe Neculaĭ*, 'I saw Nicholas.'

But when the object is a personal pronoun it precedes the verb:

*L'am vĕdut*, 'I have seen him.'
*O întreb*, 'I ask her.'
*Mi-a spus*, 'He (or she) spoke to me.

If it is wished to emphasize the assertion, the pronoun in its unabbreviated form must be repeated after the verb:

*L'am vĕdut pe el*, 'I have seen him.'
*Am vĕdut'o pe ea*, 'I have seen her.'

*Note.*—In such a case as *am vedut 'o*, the pronoun follows the verb, for the sake of euphony.

## SYNTAX.

### *The Relative Pronoun*—care, ce.

The relative pronoun *care*, *ce*, occurs more frequently in Roumanian than in English, where it is avoided by a simpler construction : thus—

*Omul de care ți-am vorbit a venit iar,*
'The man I told you of has come again.'

We cannot translate 'The man I saw,' 'The time I came,' etc., without the insertion of the relative pronoun between the subject and the verb.

### VERBS.

We have seen that verbs may be used without the subject being expressed by a personal pronoun, though the use of the latter is not incorrect:

*ar* or *eŭ ar*,    'I plough.'
*cred* or *eŭ cred*,    'I believe,' etc.

In compound tenses the auxiliary usually precedes the verb; sometimes, however, when it is a single and not a compound auxiliary, it follows the verb :

*am arat*,    *arat-am*.
*aĭ arat*,    *arat-aĭ*, etc.

When the auxiliary *aṣĭ, aĭ, ar*, etc., follows the verb, we use the second form of the infinitive:

*aṣĭ ave*,    *avere-aṣĭ*.
*aĭ ave*,    *avere-aĭ*.
*ar ave*,    *avere-ar*, etc.

But when the auxiliary is a compound one, it must always precede the verb:

*Voiŭ fi arat*, or *fi-voiŭ arat*.
*Veĭ fi arat*, ,,    *fi-veĭ* . ,,
*Va fi arat*, ,,    *fi-va* . ,,    etc.

F

The auxiliary is inseparable from the verb, except when the verb is reflective and the auxiliary follows it. In this case the pronoun, governed by the reflective verb, stands between the verb and the auxiliary:

  *eŭ m'am lupt*at, or *lupt*at-*u-m'am*.
  *tu te*-aĭ ,, ,, ,, *te*-aĭ.
  *el s'a* ,, ,, ,, *s'a*.
  *noĭ ne*-am ,, ,, ,, *ne*-am.
  *voĭ v'a*ţĭ ,, ,, ,, *v'a*ţĭ.
    etc.

Sometimes the pronoun comes between the verb and its termination; but this only rarely occurs:

  *duceţi-vĕ*, or *duce-vĕ-ţĭ*, 'be gone.'

The negative *nu* always precedes the verb:

  *Nu voiŭ ara*, ' I shall not plough.'
   etc.

The second person singular of the imperative, in the negative form, is expressed by the negative particle followed by the verb in the infinitive:

  *nu ar*a,  ' plough not.'
  *nu cred*e,  ' believe not.'
  *nu tăc*e,  ' be not silent.'
  *nu dorm*i,  ' sleep not.'
    etc.

When the interrogative form is used the subject comes after the verb:

  *Are el ce mănca?*  ' Has he anything to eat ? '

SYNTAX. 67

Only practice can teach the different cases governed by different verbs; some govern two cases:

> Mĕ vinueștĭ,
> Imĭ vinueștĭ. } 'you accuse me.'

When one verb follows another we can use either the conjunctive or the infinitive form:

> Pot să afirm că . . .
> Pot afirma că . . . } 'I can affirm that . . .'

### The use of Tenses.

In narrative we frequently substitute the present for the past, and the imperfect is very often used instead of the conditional.

The simple perfect and the simple pluperfect are used only in narrative.

In conversation we use the compound perfect when speaking of the past:

> E.g. M'am preumblat, 'I took a walk.'
> Am spus adevĕrul, 'I told the truth.'
> etc.

The past participle remains unchanged in all compound tenses of the active voice. In the passive voice only does it conform to the number and gender of its subject, being then of course only an adjective.

## ADVERBS.

The place of an adverb in a sentence is immediately following the verb which it qualifies:

  *Alexandru se află bine,*  'Alexander is well.'
  *Passerea căntă frumos,*  'The bird sings beautifully.'

But when we speak with enthusiasm the adverb precedes the verb:

*Frumos maĭ căntă passerea!* 'How beautifully the bird sings!'

When the sentence contains negatives, as *nimenĭ,* 'nobody,' *nicăirĭ,* 'nowhere,' etc., the verb must always be preceded by the negative *nu*:

  *Nimenĭ nu e a cassă,* 'Nobody is at home.'

## PREPOSITIONS.

The preposition *a* precedes the infinitive when the latter stands alone, or as subject of a sentence:

  *a ara, a crede,* etc.
  *a minţi e ruşinos,* 'It is shameful to lie.'

It is also used before the genitive singular, and in many expressions which can only be learned by practice:

  *Sunt a cassă,*  'I am at home.'
  *Se pregăteşte a plóe,* 'It is going to rain.'
  *Presimt a nenorocire,* 'I have a presentiment of coming sorrow.'
  *Miróssă a trandafir,* 'It smells like a rose.'
    etc.

The preposition *la*, 'to,' indicates direction or place whither:

| | |
|---|---|
| *Plec la Paris*, | 'I set out for Paris.' |
| *Merg la scólă*, | 'I go to school.' |

It also may indicate the place *where*, without however necessarily implying place *in*:

| | |
|---|---|
| *Sunt la bisserică*, | 'I am at church.' |
| *Sunt la grădină*, | 'I am at the park.' |
| *Poftim la massă*, | 'Please come to dinner.' |
| etc. | |

It is also used in phrases only to be learned by practice:

| | |
|---|---|
| *Arată bine la faţă*, | 'He looks well in (the) face.' |
| *Cîstigă la parale*, | 'He gains money.' |
| etc. | |

*In* has the same meaning as in English *in* or *into*:

| | |
|---|---|
| *Vino în grădină*, | 'Come into the garden.' |
| *Sunt în grădină*, | 'I am in the garden.' |

*Pe*, 'upon,' often precedes the object governed by it, when that object is a person:

| | |
|---|---|
| *Slăveste pe Dumnezeŭ*, | 'Praise God.' |
| *Invaţă pe copiĭ*, | 'He teaches the children.' |

It always precedes the object which indicates place *where*:

| | |
|---|---|
| *Şed pe scaun*, | 'I sit upon the chair.' |
| etc. | |

It is also used in many other expressions in which it is equivalent to different English prepositions:

| | |
|---|---|
| *Pe romăneşte*, | 'In Roumanian.' |
| *Pe englesește*, | 'In English,' etc. |
| *Passerea pe limba eĭ pere*, | 'The bird dies (*i.e.* meets her death) in (through) her song.' |
| *M'am preumblat pe lună*, | 'I walked in the moonlight.' |
| *Am călătorit pe sóre*, | 'I travelled in the sunshine.' |

*De,* 'of,' indicates the dependence of one noun on another, more especially when we wish to indicate the substance of a thing, or its purpose or reason:

  *Cias de* a*ur*,    'a gold watch.'
  *Pénă de scris,*   'pen for writing.'
  *Móre de sete,*   'he dies of thirst.'

We also use *de* before adverbs of number:

  *De doă ori,*   'twice.'
  *De o mie de ori,*  'thousand times.'
      etc.

*De la,* 'from,' differs from *din,* 'from,' in the same way as *la* differs from *în*.

## CONJUNCTIONS.

*Să* is used in the conjunctive mood and in the imperative.

*Că,* 'that,' is used in giving explanation:

 *Zi-ĭ că nu-s a cassă,*  'tell him I am not at home.'

This sentence could not be rendered in Roumanian without *că.*

*Că* and *ca* must be carefully distinguished, the latter suggests likeness or approximation:

*Ca mînĭ vom mur*i,   'We may die by to-morrow.'
*Aŭ fost ca la cincĭ sute de ómenĭ,* 'There were about five hundred men.'

## INTERJECTIONS.

The Interjections a*leŭ! valeŭ!* 'alas!' are used alone, and have no connection with the words which follow them.

*Vaĭ*, 'woe,' *amar* (conveying a feeling of bitterness), *ferice* (implying joy or happiness), *sĕrac* (implying pity), require the noun which follows them to be in the ablative with *de*:

<blockquote>

*Vaĭ de mine,*   'Woe to me.'

*Sĕrac de mine,*   'Poor me,' etc.

</blockquote>

But *vaĭ* and *amar* can also be used with a dative: *vaĭ mie, amar ție.*

113

www.ingramcontent.com/pod-product-compliance
Lightning Source LLC
Chambersburg PA
CBHW020227090426
42735CB00010B/1610